A Rainbow of Sound

The Instruments of the
Orchestra and Their Music

A Rainbow of Sound

By Herbert Kupferberg

ILLUSTRATED BY MORRIS WARMAN

Charles Scribner's Sons

NEW YORK

to my mother

Contents

Introduction

Many books have been written about orchestral instruments—their history, their structure, their mechanics, the technique of playing them. Yet not many attempts have been made to tell what these instruments actually contribute to the orchestra, how they fit into the beautiful tonal tapestry that constitutes a symphony.

Each instrument is more than a collection of valves and pipes, strings and resonance chambers. It is like a living organism, with a personality of its own. And often that personality reaches its fullest potential when it interacts with other personalities, in that community which we call the orchestra.

A book treating musical instruments in this light may serve several purposes.

It may help young people who are just beginning to listen to music to better appreciate the way an orchestra functions, both in its component parts and as a unit.

It may provide some elementary awareness of the art called orchestration, which is the way a composer expresses his musical ideas.

It may assist the young musician who is still learning an instrument toward a keener awareness of its individuality and the way in which it collaborates with others.

It may help guide a youngster who is trying to decide which instrument to select by giving him some idea of the potentialities, and problems, of all.

Whether the reader is a listener or a performer, it is hoped that the pages which follow will give him a greater understanding of the wonderful art of music.

The pictures in this book were taken at the Settlement Music School in Philadelphia, a remarkable institution which gives instruction annually to three thousand children of all ages. The author and the photographer wish to express their appreciation to Dr. Sol Schoenbach, the school's director, and to the young musicians who so cheerfully and patiently sat for their musical portraits.

If you walk into a symphony concert hall a few moments before the actual program begins you will hear a curious kind of music, the sound of the orchestra "tuning up." All the instruments on the stage will be busily playing, but independently of each other. The trumpets may be sounding a fanfare, the violins trying out some chords, the flutes running up and down a scale.

It is a seemingly disorganized but very pleasant sound. Indeed, a legendary Oriental gentleman, taken to his first Western orchestral concert, is supposed to have declared that the tuning up was the nicest part of the program—it reminded him so of the music of his own country.

After only a few seconds' listening, it will become apparent that the instruments spread out before you are strongly individualistic. They differ from one another drastically in size, shape, and—most important of all—sound.

The methods of playing them also differ. Some instruments are played by bowing—that is, by drawing a stick to which horsehair has been attached across a stringed box. Others are blown into. Still others are made to sound by being struck. The first group is called strings; the second, brass or woodwinds; the third, percussion.

After trying out their sounds for ten or fifteen minutes, the instruments gradually subside. Suddenly a single tone floats out of the silence, the note A played by the oboe. It is repeated by the first violinist, then taken up by the rest of the instruments. The various sounds, individualistic though they remain, are now completely in accord. Finally, the conductor enters, looks about him to make sure all the instruments are ready, and brings down his baton. Another concert has begun.

Scenes like this take place every day in concert halls throughout America. Equally important, they also occur in school auditoriums and classrooms. More and more young people are discovering the pleasure and satisfaction of playing music with others.

Most musical instruments cannot get along by themselves, any more than most people can. Music making is, and always has been, a communal art. And the orchestra is the largest and most elaborate of all musical ensembles.

The Orchestra

Its various instruments are like components of a mighty machine. Or perhaps they might better be compared to the citizens of a great musical republic, combining their capabilities and characteristics for the common good.

If the orchestra is indeed like a nation, then like a nation it has a history and a geography.

Even the most ancient peoples had orchestras of some sort. In the Bible we read: "And David and the whole house of Israel played before the Lord on all manner of instruments made of fir wood, even on harps, and on psalteries, and on timbrels, and on cornets, and on cymbals."

But the orchestra as we know it today had its beginnings about three hundred and fifty years ago. Until then, strings, woodwinds, and brasses pretty much remained by themselves, playing in small separate groups. But some imaginative early musicians began to experiment with combining them. They took the strings (first violins, second violins, violas, cellos, and basses) and began adding woodwinds to them (first the oboes and bassoons, later the flutes and clarinets). Trumpets and kettledrums came in later but were used sparingly at first because they were so much more powerful than the other instruments. Horns followed soon after, but trombones weren't admitted until the early nineteenth century. Tubas came still later. For about a hundred years now, the membership roster has remained basically fixed, although the percussion section has expanded, and various additional instruments, from the piano to the saxophone, make occasional appearances.

The "geography" of the orchestra has also changed somewhat over the years. First and second violins used to be seated on separate sides of the orchestra. Today they are grouped together at the conductor's left. The violas and cellos are at his right. In the middle are the woodwinds and brasses. At the rear, usually toward the left, is the percussion section. On the rear right, rimming the orchestra like a mountain ridge, are the double basses.

As the history has unfolded and the geography has shifted, so has the population of the orchestra expanded. One of the earliest groups, established by Louis XIV of

France in the seventeenth century, was called *Les Vingt-quatre violons du roi* ("The Twenty-four Violins of the King"). Johann Sebastian Bach, when he was musical director in Leipzig in the first half of the eighteenth century, had an orchestra of about twenty instruments. Joseph Haydn, the "father of the symphony," wrote for an orchestra of about twenty-five. Ludwig van Beethoven, probably the greatest symphonist of all time, usually had no more than forty.

Today's orchestras are considerably larger. Some of our great symphony organizations, such as those in Boston, Chicago, Cleveland, New York, and Philadelphia, number more than a hundred players. A good-sized high school orchestra can have fifty or sixty.

No matter what its size, an orchestra must maintain a good balance between sections and between individuals. Just as every person has his own voice, so does each instrument have its own distinctive tone color, generally known by the French word *timbre*. Each brings its own quality—the suppleness of violins, the richness of violas and cellos, the brilliance of trumpets, the grandeur of trombones, the poignance of oboes, the alternating melancholy and comedy of bassoons, the celestial quality of harps, the romanticism of horns, the rhythmic authority of kettledrums.

To let each instrument's voice be heard at the right time in the right place is partially the job of the conductor. But it also is the responsibility of the performer himself. For behind each instrument sits a human being—a man or a woman, a boy or a girl. An orchestra, after all, is made up not only of instruments but of people. And it is the players who must bring to life their flutes and violins, cellos and English horns. They must possess both the technique to play their instruments and the musicianship to grasp a composer's ideas and intentions.

To play well in an orchestra is no easy task. Good musicians have always realized this. Back in 1756, Leopold Mozart, the father of the great composer Wolfgang Amadeus Mozart, wrote: "Decide now for yourself whether a good orchestral violinist is not of far higher value than one who is purely a solo player. The latter can play everything according to his wishes, and arrange the style of the performance as he desires, or even for the convenience of his hand. But the former must possess the dexterity to understand and interpret the thoughts of different composers. . . . A solo player can, without great understanding of music, usually play his concertos fairly well—yea, even with distinction—but a good orchestral violinist must have deep insight into the whole art of musical composition."

Leopold Mozart's words about violinists apply equally well to other orchestral musicians. Let us now examine all the players and their instruments, section by section and one by one, to see what each contributes to that beautiful rainbow of sound which we call orchestral music.

Strings

The strings are the backbone of the orchestra. It's even possible to have an entire orchestra made up of strings, though it will lack the color and variety of one that also includes woodwinds, brasses, and percussion. Still, there are many works for strings alone, such as Wolfgang Amadeus Mozart's *Eine Kleine Nachtmusik* (A Little Night Music) and Peter Ilyich Tchaikovsky's Serenade for Strings.

There are also music combinations without strings, ranging from small woodwind ensembles to large brass bands. These can make colorful and exciting music. But only a full symphony orchestra can produce a complete spectrum of sound and color.

To call the strings a "family" is very fitting. Its four main members closely resemble each other in everything but size. In fact, the violin shape is one of the most distinctive and beautiful forms ever devised by man. It is not difficult to imagine the violin, viola, cello, and bass, when placed side by side, as four brothers and sisters lined up in size places.

No family in the orchestra is as involved in so many different types of activity as the strings. They seem tireless, for they are almost always in action. They can play the leading melody themselves or, with equal grace, provide an accompaniment for some other instrument. They can be played with a bow or plucked with the fingers (*pizzicato*). They can be muted by placing a simple attachment over their bridge, or they can sing out full voice. Except for the basses, they can express almost any emotion and create many moods. More than half of the orchestra consists of strings, making them by far the biggest, as well as the busiest, of all the sections.

Just as strings outnumber all other instruments, so do violins outnumber all other strings. They usually make up about one-third the total personnel of the orchestra.

The instrument itself is made of wood, varnished to a handsome finish. The strings are of gut or metal. It is a complicated instrument to build, with more than seventy parts. The art of making stringed instruments has not improved since the seventeenth century. That is why, although wind players like new instruments, violinists prefer old ones.

An orchestral violinist hardly ever gets to lay his bow down during a concert. In many symphonies, overtures, and tone poems the violins play almost continuously, with only an occasional "rest." Composers like to entrust them with their most beautiful ideas because, like the human voice, they are capable of so many shades of expression. An orchestra really cannot exist without violins, although composers have tried it on occasion. Bach omitted violins from his *Brandenburg* Concerto no. 6 in B-flat—no one knows why. The music is still beautiful, though dark in hue. A French composer named Étienne Méhul did the

Violin

Sharp violins proclaim
Their jealous pangs and desperation,
Fury, frantic indignation,
Depths of pains, and height of
   passion.

JOHN DRYDEN
A Song for St. Cecelia's Day (1687)

same thing in his opera *Uthal*, leaving the main string part to the viola. At its conclusion André Gréty, another composer, who was in the audience, exclaimed: "I'd give a hundred francs to hear a violin!"

Violins are divided into "firsts" and "seconds." Theoretically there should be an equal number of each, but usually there are a few more firsts.

It's unfortunate that the expression "playing second fiddle" has taken on a derogatory meaning. Calling some violins "first" and others "second" doesn't mean that they are first- and second-class citizens of the orchestra. The purpose, rather, is to provide a greater depth and flexibility to the sound. Firsts and seconds sometimes play in unison. More often there is an octave between them, with the firsts having the higher notes and the seconds the lower. Sometimes they part ways completely, adding a new dimension to the sound.

A special place in the orchestra is held by the leader of the first violins. He is called the concertmaster and sits immediately to the left of the conductor in the "first chair." He serves as the conductor's deputy in many ways.

The concertmaster is the most skillful of all the violinists in the orchestra. He is often called upon to play solo passages of great difficulty. Nicolai Rimsky-Korsakov's *Scheherazade*, Richard Strauss's *Ein Heldenleben*, and Camille Saint-Saëns's *Danse Macabre* are among the dozens of works that almost turn a concertmaster into a concert soloist. No wonder that when a concert ends, the conductor so often shakes hands with his concertmaster.

Viola

To regard the viola simply as an overgrown violin is a mistake. True, they both have the same shape and structure, and they are both held under the chin and played similarly. But the viola is larger, and plays a fifth lower than the violin.

The rich, deep-toned viola is a newly liberated instrument. In the early years of the orchestra, viola players were musicians who couldn't make the grade as violinists. Many were old and doddering. Composers were afraid to give them important or prominent passages in their symphonies. Instead, the instrument was used to "fill in the middle."

Mozart was one of the first to trust the viola. He himself could play almost every instrument, but he preferred to occupy the viola chair when playing with his friends in a string quartet. He said he liked to "sit in the middle" and hear what was going on around him.

Every skillful violinist can in a few weeks acquire the ability to play the viola fairly well; but the true virtuoso of the viola must study his instrument long and faithfully.

ALBERT LAVIGNAC
Music and Musicians (1895)

In Mozart's great Symphony no. 40 in G Minor, he gives the opening phrase to the violas. Technically, this is only an accompaniment passage, over which the violins play the main melody. But it is the throbbing viola pattern that sets the intense emotional mood of the entire work. Years later another great composer, Felix Mendelssohn, praised this passage and said it was impossible to reproduce its peculiar viola coloration upon the piano.

The thick-stringed viola has never had the appeal of more flexible and flashy instruments. But musicians have come to recognize its solid virtues and distinctive tone. Mendelssohn, who learned much from Mozart, let the viola color dominate the slow movement of his Symphony no. 4 in A (*Italian*).

The first violist, like the concertmaster, has a number of outstanding solo passages in works like Hector Berlioz's *Harold in Italy* and Richard Strauss's *Don Quixote*. The violist, no less than his neighbor the violinist, must be a master of his instrument.

Like the violin, the cello is an orchestral workhorse. It provides a sturdy bass, it helps the viola to fill the middle range, and it often surges to the fore itself in song-like passages. In range and flexibility, it approximates the human voice, particularly the male voice (the violin is closer to the female voice). When a song or operatic aria is transcribed for orchestra, it is likely to be the cello which is given the vocal line.

Haydn and Mozart treated the cello with respect. But it was Beethoven who, so to speak, put the cello on its feet as an independent orchestral instrument. He gave it some of his most important and original utterances—for example, the bold opening theme of the Symphony no. 3 in E-flat (the *Eroica*) and the noble "Ode to Joy" melody of the Symphony no. 9 in D Minor (the *Choral*). At the start of the second movement of his Symphony no. 5 in C Minor

Cello

I hear the violoncello,
('tis the young man's heart's
   complaint).

> Walt Whitman
> *Song of Myself* (1855)

he showed how sonorously the cello and viola sounds could be combined in unison.

Composers ever since have turned the cello into one of their most eloquent orchestral spokesmen. The famous theme of Franz Schubert's Symphony no. 8 in B Minor (the *Unfinished*) is a cello melody. So is the wistful opening of the third movement of Johannes Brahms's Symphony no. 3 in F. The instrument also has many great solo passages, such as the andante of Brahms's Piano Concerto no. 2 in B-flat, where it sings a melody so beautiful that it gently nudges the piano itself into the background. In Saint-Saëns's *Carnival of the Animals*, the cello plays the graceful and sinuous theme of "The Swan."

The cello is so large that it must be held between the knees and played in a seated position. But although the instrument itself is bulkier than the violin and viola, the bow with which it is played is shorter.

Interestingly, top cellists often develop into successful conductors. Arturo Toscanini, perhaps the greatest conductor of the twentieth century, was a cellist in his youth. He first became famous at the age of nineteen when he was called upon to take over an orchestra whose conductor was unable to appear. He left the cellist's chair to do so, and never returned. But to the end of his life he never lost the habit of humming the cello line of every work he conducted.

Double Bass

Every concert-goer has observed the ring of double basses at one side of the orchestra. This ponderous, friendly-looking instrument is known by a variety of names: double bass, contrabass, bass viol, bass, bull fiddle, and doghouse! Whatever it's called, its basic job in the orchestra remains the same, to give a solid underpinning to the harmonies and to accentuate the rhythm.

So large is the instrument that it must be played either while standing up or seated on a high stool. In early years, the double bass was held in low regard. It didn't even rate a line of its own in the score. But Beethoven changed all that, as he changed so many other old ideas about orchestration. His symphonies give a prominent role to the double basses, though they often have to share the spotlight with other deep-voiced instruments like the cellos and bassoons. They dance like elephants in Beethoven's Symphony no. 5 in C Minor, and they play up a storm in his Symphony no. 6 in F (the *Pastoral*).

Beethoven's affection for the double bass led another composer, named Carl Maria von Weber, to write a satirical essay. Weber depicted all the orchestral instruments holding a protest meeting to denounce Beethoven for making them work so hard and giving them so many unheard-of tasks. The double bass was particularly indignant. "Instead of letting me behave in a quiet and orderly manner as befits my dignity," he complained, "this composer makes me skip about like the giddiest young violin!" The instruments raised such a fuss that the janitor rushed in. The only way he could silence them was to threaten to ask Mr. Beethoven to write another symphony unless they quieted down!

The double bass has come into its own today in jazz and rock music. But its role in the symphony is important, too. An orchestra without basses is as unthinkable as a room without a floor.

The first string that the Musician usually touches is the Bass, when he intends to put all in tune. God also plays upon this string first, when he sets the soul in tune for himself.

JOHN BUNYAN
The Pilgrim's Progress (1678)

The history of the harp goes back to the Old Testament. In the First Book of Samuel it is written: "And it came to pass, when the evil spirit from God was upon Saul, that David took a harp and played with his hand: so Saul was refreshed."

This soothing effect continues in the modern orchestra. A few notes plucked on the harp can contribute a celestial, radiant, or dreamy feeling to the orchestral texture.

Despite its ancient lineage, the harp is a rather recent addition to the orchestra. Even Beethoven rarely wrote for it. The great turning point in its history came in 1810 when Sebastian Erard, a Frenchman, added pedals. These vastly increased the range of the forty-seven strings. There also is a modern, simplified version of the instrument called the troubadour harp, with fewer strings and no pedals. It is used mainly for training and teaching young harpists.

If King David were suddenly to reappear and visit a concert hall, he might recognize, alone among the instruments, the sound of the harp. But he would be astounded by the variety of effects it may achieve nowadays.

Most orchestras have two harps, though some compositions call for as many as four. Berlioz, in his *Fantastic* Symphony, was one of the first composers to give the harps spectacular solo passages. The instrument has also been used imaginatively by composers of the romantic and impressionistic schools, including Liszt, Tchaikovsky, Strauss, Debussy, and Ravel. The *glissando* effect, in which the finger slides rapidly over the strings, is like none other in music.

Besides being a distinctive solo instrument, the harp is a good "team player." It blends well with other instruments, especially the flute and other members of the woodwind family.

Harp

Of course no one ever writes out the correct nomenclature of all the strings touched by the harpist in a glissando. Life is too short.

CECIL FORSYTH
Orchestration (1936)

Woodwinds

If the strings provide the basic picture of a symphonic composition, the woodwinds color it in. The four primary woodwinds—flute, oboe, clarinet, and bassoon—are at their best as orchestral instruments. Heard individually over long periods, they can become somewhat tiring to the ear. But in combination with others they flourish brightly, adding marvelous hues and glints of color to the musical fabric.

Originally all woodwind instruments were made of wood. Today other materials are sometimes used. Just as the human hand plays the string and percussion instruments, so does the human breath activate the woodwinds and the brasses. In the winds the player sets a column of air in motion with his lips and controls its sound by stopping holes with his fingers, generally using keys provided for the purpose.

Most woodwind instruments have small reeds of cane affixed to their mouthpieces. These vibrate as the player blows, thus giving the instrument its characteristic tone. Woodwind players cut and care for their own reeds.

Usually woodwinds come in pairs, like Noah's animals. But some works call for four of each kind or, in extreme cases, even more. Only about ten to fifteen percent of an orchestra consists of woodwinds. But so vivid are their hues that they leave an indelible imprint. Their original role in the orchestra was merely to reinforce the strings. But composers like Haydn and Mozart gave them short solo passages of great beauty, and these were gradually lengthened out in the post-Beethoven, or "romantic," era. Newer and more specialized woodwinds were admitted to the orchestra, further extending the color spectrum. Among these are the piccolo, the English horn, the bass clarinet, and the contrabassoon.

Like violinists, woodwind players are divided into firsts and seconds. The distinction is important, because when the music calls for a wind solo, it can be played by only one player. So the first oboe or flute will get to play many beau-

24

tiful solo melodies while the second remains in a supporting role. Naturally, this "exposed" position puts a much greater responsibility on the first-chair player. A really good second-chair player will also be able to play solo passages if need be.

Man has been extracting music from pipes since the beginning of time. However, the modern flute is a far cry from the primitive device known to the Greeks and Egyptians. It is even different from the orchestral instrument played through the eighteenth century.

In 1832 a German technician named Theobald Boehm invented a system of mechanical keys and stoppers for the flute. This made it as controllable and precise as a fine watch.

Ancient flutes were blown from the end and had open holes along the side which the player stopped with his fingers. This system survives today in an instrument called the recorder, which is fun to play, but is never found in the standard symphony orchestra, although it performs valuable musical services in other groups. Today's flute, usually made of silver or some other metal, has its mouthpiece on the side. It is called a transverse flute.

Flute

And the staff was bored and drilled for those
Who on a flute could play;
And thus the merry Pilgrim had
His music on the way.

ROBERT SOUTHEY
"The Pilgrim to Compostella" (1837)

The flute is the only woodwind without reeds to color its sound. Its pure tone comes entirely from the vibration of the column of air inside the tube. Everything is up to the player. He or she must project a thin, steady jet stream of air across the opening. The position of the lips, called in French *embouchure*, is all-important. Famous flutist William Kincaid once said the flute was "the easiest instrument to play badly and the hardest to play well."

The flute is agile and versatile. Its clear, limpid tone can create or change the mood of an entire piece all by itself. In the storm scene of Beethoven's *Pastoral* Symphony, there is a little ascending figure for flute which seems to depict a patch of blue sky opening in a rift among the passing clouds. Mendelssohn in his *Fingal's Cave*, or *Hebrides*, Overture used two flutes to suggest a crest of spray upon the breaking waves of the sea.

The flute does a dance of its own in Tchaikovsky's *Nutcracker* Suite; it languidly opens Claude Debussy's *Afternoon of a Faun*; it safeguards the hero and heroine of Mozart's opera *The Magic Flute* through the perils of fire and water. To be a flutist is to know some of music's noblest passages.

The flute has a smaller brother called the piccolo, a word which means "little" in Italian. The piccolo is half the size of the flute but is played in exactly the same way. It emits a shrill and piercing sound that can be comical, brilliant, or martial in effect. Although the piccolo makes infrequent appearances, they are likely to be memorable.

27 / *Woodwinds*

The oboe is a difficult and treacherous instrument to play. But it has one of the orchestra's most recognizable and expressive voices. Its mouthpiece consists of two thin tongues of reed with a small space between, almost like a slightly flattened straw. The instrument itself is a graceful black tube covered with silvery keys and rods.

More than the other woodwinds, the oboe must be played with a limited amount of breath. The player has to constantly hold back, and even to exhale (quietly!) during pauses. No wonder there is a joking definition of the oboe as "an ill wind that nobody blows good."

Oboe

A boxen hautboy, loud and sweet of sound,
All varnished and with brazen ringlets round,
I to the victor give.

AMBROSE PHILIPS
Pastorals, VI (1709)

Originally the instrument was known as the *hautbois*, French for "high wood." It was one of the first woodwinds to become a full-fledged instrument of the orchestra. Since the oboe is difficult to tune, it plays the diapason, the standard pitch of the note A, to which all the other instruments must tune before every concert.

But the oboe's moment of glory is not limited to that one note. Its reedy, penetrating voice can depict pathos, innocence, nostalgia, yearning, and many other feelings. Christoph Willibald von Gluck gave it hauntingly beautiful music in the "Scene of the Departed Spirits" in his opera *Orpheus and Eurydice*. Beethoven used it for a brief moment of repose amid the headlong drama of the first movement of his Symphony no. 5. Its power to convey a feeling of sadness is shown in the "Funeral March" of Beethoven's *Eroica* Symphony and in the slow movement of Schubert's great Symphony no. 9 in C Major.

The oboe blends admirably with other instruments. Haydn and Mozart included some beautiful dialogues between oboes and violins in their symphonies. It also goes well with the other winds and the brasses.

A larger, deeper-voiced version of the oboe is the English horn. Its wooden tube is longer and somewhat wider and flares out at the end into a "bell," or expanded opening. The mouthpiece is slightly bent to enable the player to hold it more comfortably.

This may account for its name, for, as is often pointed out, the English horn is neither English nor a horn. But the French call it *cor anglé* (bent horn), and this may have been translated carelessly years ago into English horn (*cor Anglais*). In any case, the English horn, with its hauntingly deep notes, plays some remarkably lovely symphonic melodies, including those in César Franck's Symphony in D Minor, Jan Sibelius's *The Swan of Tuonela*, and most famous of all, the "Goin' Home" largo of Anton Dvořák's Symphony no. 9 in E Minor, *From the New World*.

The clarinet was the last of the basic woodwind instruments to reach the orchestra. But it probably is the most flexible and eloquent of all. In concert bands, which have no string instruments at all, the clarinet takes the place of the violin, so wide is its range and versatility.

A good orchestral clarinetist will probably play more than one instrument, since the clarinet comes in several different keys. The most useful are B-flat and A-natural. The clarinet has only a single reed fastened to its rather thick mouthpiece, as contrasted to the double reed of the oboe. Its deepest register, called the "chalumeau," can produce mysterious and spectral effects. Its middle range is mellow and warm. And its upper notes can be either comical or startling.

Mozart was delighted with the vibrancy of the clarinet and used it whenever he could. The third movement of his

Clarinet

Ah, if we only had some clarinets, too! You cannot imagine the glorious effect of a symphony with flutes, oboes, and clarinets!

WOLFGANG AMADEUS MOZART
in a letter to his father
(December 3, 1778)

Symphony no. 39 in E-flat contains one of the earliest (and most beautiful) of all orchestral clarinet solos. Mozart also wrote a lovely concerto and a quintet featuring the instrument. Mendelssohn gave it a stirring, swirling solo in his Symphony no. 3 in A Minor (the *Scotch*). The slow, sad melody that opens Tchaikovsky's Symphony no. 5 in E Minor is played by two clarinets in unison. In Strauss's tone poem *Till Eulenspiegel's Merry Pranks* the rascally hero dies on the scaffold to the high squeal of the E-flat clarinet. Although a latecomer, the clarinet has made for itself an indispensable place in the orchestra.

The bass clarinet is a larger replica of the clarinet. It is pitched an octave lower and is so large that it usually rests on a prong on the floor. The American composer Ferde Grofé set off its dark tones neatly in the "On the Trail" section of his *Grand Canyon* Suite. The bass clarinet seems to be growing in popularity. It can contribute a feeling of solemnity, mystery, or grotesqueness. It's not a very cheerful instrument but is a useful one.

31 / *Woodwinds*

The bassoon has a reputation as the clown of the orchestra. Beethoven used it to wheeze out a peasant dance in his *Pastoral* Symphony, Mendelssohn to imitate the braying of a donkey in his *Midsummer Night's Dream* Overture, and Paul Dukas to depict a broom carrying buckets of water in *The Sorcerer's Apprentice*.

But this generous-sized instrument can do more than make jokes. The bassoon is the bass of the woodwind quartet. Like the oboe, it has a double reed. If it were constructed in a straight line, it would be eight feet long. To make it easier to handle, its tube has been bent double on itself. The air blown into it goes down one pipe, makes a U-turn, and comes up the other. It has a bent tubular mouthpiece, or crook, about two-thirds of the way up. It certainly is one of the more oddly shaped instruments of the orchestra. The Italians thought it resembled a bundle

Bassoon

By simply assassinating less than a dozen men, I could leave London without a single orchestral wind instrument player of the first rank. . . . Imagine a city with five million inhabitants and only one satisfactory bassoon player!

GEORGE BERNARD SHAW
The World (May 28, 1890)

of sticks, or "fagotto"—the name which it is often called in orchestral scores.

In its early years in the orchestra it served mostly to reinforce the bass line of the strings. It still performs the valuable function of filling in the harmony. But since it can give a feeling of dignity or pathos, as well as a chuckling good humor, it also has some notable solo passages. The great modern composer Igor Stravinsky made wonderful use of the bassoon. In *The Firebird* he used it to sing a "Berceuse," a cradle song, over an accompaniment of muted strings and harp. In his *The Rite of Spring*, the work that revolutionized twentieth-century music, the bassoon performs the unaccompanied opening figure, playing in its upper compass—an extraordinary passage.

But it was Beethoven who relied on the bassoon most of all. His symphonies, his Violin Concerto in D, and many other works are shot through with prominent bassoon passages. He is said to have loved the bassoon above all other instruments. Orchestral players can ask for no better friend.

A companion piece of the bassoon is the contrabassoon. This is a really mammoth instrument that would measure sixteen feet if straightened out. The double bassoon, as it is sometimes called, is doubled back four times upon itself and is the deepest-voiced of all the regulation orchestral instruments. Haydn used it in his oratorio *The Creation* to represent footsteps at the words "by heavy beasts the ground is trod." Brahms gave it a noble and dignified passage in the last movement of his Symphony no. 1 in C Minor. When called upon, the contrabassoon can certainly make its presence felt.

Questions arise about this instrument. Is it a woodwind or a brass? Is it "popular" or "classical"? Probably the best answer to both questions is "both." The saxophone was invented around 1840 by a Belgian musician named Adolphe Sax. He loved to produce musical hybrids. Among his other inventions were the saxhorn and the saxotromba.

The saxophone has a single-reed mouthpiece, like that of a clarinet, and a metal body. It comes in soprano, alto, tenor, and baritone varieties and has a distinctively mellow and flexible tone. The saxophone has led a flourishing career in jazz and military bands. Its acceptance by classical musicians has been slower.

Nevertheless, most symphony orchestras have at least one "sax" on call. Richard Strauss, in a seldom-played work entitled *Sinfonia Domestica*, calls for a quartet of saxophones. Maybe that is one reason why that work is seldom played. French composers seem especially attached to the saxophone. None has written for it more beautifully than Georges Bizet, the composer of *Carmen*, in his suite *L'Arlésienne*.

The saxophone is a good example of an orchestra instrument which, while not a full-fledged member of the orchestral family, is a welcome guest. It also provides us with a convenient transition from the woodwind to the brass instruments.

Saxophone

Drum on your drums, batter on your banjos,
sob on the long cool winding saxophones.

CARL SANDBURG
Jazz Fantasia (1920)

Brass

No other section of the orchestra approaches the brasses for sheer brilliance and splendor of sound. Perhaps this was why they were accepted so slowly into membership, almost as if the other instruments were reluctant to admit them because they knew they would be overshadowed.

For all their power, the brasses have their limitations. They lack the versatility of the strings and the subtlety of the woodwinds. Many composers reserve them for climactic moments, although there are unforgettable solo passages for brass instruments, too.

Unlike the woodwinds, the brasses have no reeds. The sound depends entirely upon the player's lips. Originally there were no valves on trumpets and French horns, the first brasses to enter the orchestra. Today valves have been added, making them easier to play.

A full symphony orchestra may have two or three trumpets, four French horns, three trombones, and one tuba— like the woodwinds, adding up to about fifteen percent of the total personnel. This small group is the tonal power-house of the orchestra. Composers must know when to let the brasses dominate the sound of the entire ensemble, and when to hold them in check. They must also know how to blend the rich harmonies of the brasses with other instruments.

String players sometimes complain that, while they must work from start to finish of a symphony, the brasses play only in spurts. In fact, sometimes an instrument like the tuba may be excused from an entire concert.

However, brass players argue that while they are called upon to play less, they are always put in an exposed position. If a violin plays a false note, few besides his fellow violinists are likely to notice it. Even an error by a woodwind may not be glaring. But let a trumpeter "crack" on a high note, or a horn player emit a "burble," and the whole world knows it at once. Brass players must be musicians of

courage and confidence.

French Horn

It obviously is a horn, but why French? The best answer seems to be that this graceful instrument is a descendant of the ancient French hunting horn, which used to echo through the forests on royal hunts. A French composer, Jean Baptiste Lully, is generally credited with having first introduced it into the orchestra in 1664. Nevertheless, modern musicians are dropping the word "French" and usually refer to the instrument simply as the "horn."

Whatever they're called, these shiny, coiled, circular instruments are as pleasing to the eye as to the ear. The horn is the only "left-handed" instrument. The player uses the fingers of his left hand to manipulate the valves. He inserts his right hand into the bell of the instrument—a technique called "stopping," which actually produces extra notes.

Horns may be played in several keys, the most customary being F and B-flat. The four horns of the orchestra operate in pairs. Numbers one and three play the high notes; numbers two and four the low. They must learn to work together as smoothly as a football backfield.

This kind of harmony is not easy to achieve, but the results can be magnificent. The horn has the power to radiate warmth through the entire orchestra. It is the most subtle and adaptable of all the brasses. In Weber's overture to *Der Freischütz* it is serene; in Tchaikovsky's Fifth Symphony, lyrical; in Richard Strauss's tone poem *Don Juan*, exuberant. In Richard Wagner's *Siegfried Idyll*, it gives off its most elemental sound of all—a hunting call. Perhaps its supreme moment in symphonic literature comes at the very opening of Schubert's great Symphony no. 9 in C Major. Here, for seven measures, two horns in C, completely unaccompanied, play the theme that sets the mood for this entire noble work.

At the beginning of the [nineteenth] century . . . the horn tone, which soars over all barriers with which the classic style surrounded it, became the symbol of the modern orchestra, which it saturated with its glorious sonority.

PAUL HENRY LANG
Music in Western Civilization (1941)

Ever since Joshua demolished the walls of Jericho with its piercing blast, the trumpet has been one of mankind's best known and most useful instruments. It was the first of the brasses to come into the orchestra. Bach gave it a spectacularly difficult part in his *Brandenburg* Concerto no. 2 in F. George Frideric Handel had it engage in an exciting duet with the human voice in the aria "And the trumpet shall sound" in his *Messiah*.

The modern trumpet, equipped with valves, is far more flexible than the instrument of Bach's and Handel's time, not to mention Joshua's. Its mouthpiece is cup-shaped. To play it—or any of the other brasses—the performer's lips stretch across the mouthpiece and act as vibrating reeds.

Trumpets may be played in a number of keys. They also are capable of many sounds besides martial fanfares. An expert trumpeter can mute his instrument for a gentle effect.

Trumpet

If the trumpet give an uncertain sound,
who shall prepare himself to the battle?

The First Epistle of Paul to the Corinthians

Simply because the instrument's tone is so powerful, a trumpeter puts his reputation on the line with almost every note he blows. Two particularly stirring trumpet passages occur in Gioacchino Rossini's *William Tell* Overture (made famous by the Lone Ranger) and in Beethoven's *Leonore* Overture no. 3, written for his opera *Fidelio*. In both these episodes, the trumpet announces that rescue is at hand for the hero. Equally difficult and challenging is the single opening note, relatively faint and subdued, which the trumpeter must play in Wagner's *Rienzi* Overture.

In military bands and in some school orchestras, the trumpet is sometimes replaced by the cornet. They resemble each other in appearance, although the cornet is shorter. It also is easier to play, and its tone is less brilliant and more mellow. However, the ringing sound and brighter color of the trumpet make it the preferable instrument in a symphony orchestra.

Unlike most instruments, the trombones' entry into the symphony orchestra can be dated exactly. Their debut took place on December 22, 1808, in Vienna, when Beethoven introduced them in the finale of his Symphony no. 5 in C Minor. He wished to produce a sudden outburst of triumph and splendor. Trombones have been supplying these characteristics in symphonic music ever since. Generally an orchestra has two tenor trombones and one bass.

Although the trombone was accepted late into the orchestra, it has a very ancient history. It was once known as the sackbut, and it has always been elongated in shape and made up of sliding tubes. It can provide sounds ranging from an angry staccato rasp to rich, religious-like sonorities. For pure solemnity no other instrument can match it. For an example, listen to the three opening chords of Mozart's

Trombone

Directed by the will of a master, the trombones can chant like a choir of priests, threaten, utter gloomy sighs, a mournful lament, or a bright hymn of glory.

HECTOR BERLIOZ
Traité d'instrumentation (1844)

overture to *The Magic Flute*. Mozart also employed trombones to back up the menacing words of the Stone Statue in *Don Giovanni*.

Berlioz, the French composer who loved to write for huge orchestras, was the trombone's best friend. He called it "the true chief of that race of wind instruments which I distinguish as epic." His works are full of powerful trombone passages. Wagner also made good use of the instrument, as in his *Tannhäuser* Overture and the prelude to Act III of *Lohengrin*.

Symphony trombonists are expected to play each note cleanly and distinctly. Jazz trombonists, on the other hand, "slide" or "scoop" from note to note. Attempts have been made over the years to equip trombones with valves instead of slides. "The structure of the trombone hasn't changed in four hundred years," conductor Leopold Stokowski once complained. Nevertheless, players and audiences alike seem to prefer to leave this noble instrument as it is.

This huge instrument, the bass of the brass section, was developed in the nineteenth century. There are both tenor and bass tubas. They can roll out deep tones in a manner either majestic or mysterious.

The tuba's main function is to provide a support for the harmonic weight of the brasses. But it has some impressive moments of its own, such as representing a bear in Stravinsky's ballet *Petrouchka,* or impersonating Sancho Panza in Richard Strauss's tone poem *Don Quixote.* Wagner was fascinated by the tuba, as by all deep brass instruments. In his opera *Siegfried* the tuba represents the dragon Fafnir prior to its demise at the hands of the hero. Most often, it teams up with the other brass instruments.

Tuba

People never write pretty melodies for tubas. It just isn't done.
GEORGE KLEINSINGER
and PAUL TRIPP
Tubby the Tuba (1945)

The tuba is unwieldy in size and occasionally unpredictable in sound. But in the hands of an expert player, it can lend a dignified and even a gentle quality to music.

According to one story, the great conductor Arturo Toscanini, at a rehearsal of Wagner's *Faust* Overture, asked the tuba player: "Please play that passage again." Twice more he repeated his request. Finally the player asked what was wrong. "Nothing," replied the Maestro. "Only I never heard anything so beautiful."

Percussion

"What do you have to know to play the cymbals?" a music student is supposed to have once asked Sir Malcolm Sargent, the British conductor. "Nothing," he replied, "except when."

That's a slight exaggeration, of course, but timing *is* essential. A single misplaced percussion note can ruin an entire performance. But percussionists must also bring skill and sensitivity to their playing. Although all percussion instruments are played by being struck, each produces a different sound. They contribute brilliance, variety, and color to the orchestra, as well as rhythm. Percussionists even get to play melodies at times. They must be excellent musicians.

Some symphonic compositions call for no percussion at all. One example is Mozart's Symphony no. 40 in G Minor. Usually, however, there is at least a set of timpani, or kettledrums. Some works, especially the more modern ones, have a whole army of percussion instruments, often called the "battery."

The timpani are hollow hemispheres of copper covered with a "head" of tight parchment. They resemble inverted teakettles, from which comes their English name, kettledrums. The player strikes them with sticks that are tipped by a felt knob. He can vary their pitch by tightening the surface of the drum, usually by means of a pedal. This ability to change pitch sets the kettledrums apart from most other percussion instruments. Sometimes during a concert you will see the timpanist leaning over his instrument as he tunes it.

The timpanist usually has long "rests," or periods of silence. He is supposed to "count" the passing measures, but many drummers either know the music so well or follow the conductor so closely that they don't bother. There is even a story about one Viennese timpanist who used to go out for refreshments and return just in time to strike the drum. Actually, other players besides percussionists have a way of slipping in and out when they have idle moments.

The kettledrum is a great rhythmic instrument, but it can do many other things besides beat out the time. It's the kettledrum that helps provide the surprise in Haydn's *Surprise* Symphony no. 94 in G, with an unexpectedly loud chord intended, so the story goes, to awaken sleepy listeners. Beethoven made more serious use of the instrument. In his Symphony no. 5 it provides a mysterious, suspenseful transition from the third movement to the fourth. In the Scherzo of his Symphony no. 9, the *Choral*, it has a distinctive solo figure that it reiterates dramatically.

In Berlioz's *Fantastic* Symphony the kettledrum depicts a thunderstorm realistically. In Brahms's Symphony no. 1 in C Minor, it pulses through the opening like a great heartbeat. Timpanists have some great moments.

Timpani

The drum is in hands that will know how to beat it well enough.
MIGUEL DE CERVANTES
Don Quixote (1605)

Back in 1794 Haydn included triangle, cymbals, and "tamburo grande" (big drum) in his Symphony no. 100 in G, the *Military*. It was one of the first instances of a composer employing the "battery" to provide special effects. Nowadays such instruments have become more or less commonplace in the orchestra. Here are some of the most frequently encountered:

Bells. Long steel tubes that hang from a wooden frame. They give a bell-like sound when struck. Russian composers seem to like them especially, as in the joyous clanging that climaxes Tchaikovsky's *1812* Overture.

Castanets. A clicking device much used in Spanish music. Bizet uses them in his opera *Carmen.*

Celesta. A bell instrument operated by a keyboard. It has a dreamy, sweet, soft tone, and can, of course, play melodies. An exquisite example is the "Dance of the Sugar Plum Fairy" in Tchaikovsky's *Nutcracker.*

Cymbals. Probably the most familiar percussion instrument, after the timpani. They are a pair of large, round, metallic plates. Clashed together they add to the brilliance of an orchestral climax. Or one may be suspended from a stand and tapped lightly for more subtle effects.

Drums. Three military types are sometimes used in the symphony orchestra: snare drum (sometimes called side drum), tenor drum, and bass drum.

Glockenspiel. A set of steel plates that produce delightful chimes when struck by a wooden hammer.

Gong. A heavy, hanging plate that gives off a deep, reverberating, Oriental sound. It is also known as the tam-tam.

Tambourine. A kind of a hand-drum with little metal jingles attached. It may be heard in the "Arabian Dance" of the *Nutcracker.*

Triangle. A small steel bar bent into a triangle which gives a clear, ringing tone when struck. Franz Liszt gave it such an important part in his Piano Concerto no. 1 in E-flat that this work has become known as the "Triangle Concerto."

Woodblocks. Hollow blocks that produce sounds of indefinite pitch when struck together.

Battery

Praise him upon the loud cymbals:
  praise him upon the high sounding
    cymbals.
Let everything that hath breath
  praise the Lord.

Psalm 150

Xylophone. This familiar melodic instrument consists of wooden slabs arranged in two rows which are struck by mallets. A good player can produce some spectacular effects. In Saint-Saëns's *Danse Macabre* the xylophone imitates the sound of skeletons dancing.

As long as this list is, it is still incomplete. Other percussion devices include the anvil, the rattle, the tom-tom, the whip, and the wind-machine. Still others may be on the way, for the battery is one section of the orchestra that always seems ready to accept new members.

There's an old tradition for a keyboard player to be included in the ranks of the orchestra. In Bach's day a harpsichord usually filled out the harmony.

Today when a pianist appears with an orchestra, it generally is as a soloist, playing a concerto. But in some works, a piano is incorporated right into the orchestral fabric. Two examples are Richard Strauss's *Le Bourgeois gentilhomme* Suite and Béla Bartók's Dance Suite for Orchestra. Saint-Saëns's *Carnival of the Animals* calls for *two* pianos.

Is the piano a percussion or a string instrument? Actually, it is a combination of both, with felt hammers that strike its metallic strings to produce its distinctive sound. As well as being the supreme solo instrument, the piano can be a valuable member of the orchestra. That is why many orchestras include a staff pianist on their rosters.

Another keyboard instrument that sometimes joins the orchestra's ranks is the organ. In Richard Strauss's tone

Piano

'Tis wonderful how soon a piano gets into a log-hut on the frontier.
RALPH WALDO EMERSON
Society and Solitude:
Civilization (1870)

poem *Also sprach Zarathustra*, it's the low throb of the organ that provides the eerie opening music that has become famous in the movie *2001: A Space Odyssey*. The organ plays such an important part in Saint-Saëns's Symphony no. 3 in C Minor that this work has become known as the *Organ Symphony*.

In recent years electronic keyboard instruments have begun to make appearances in orchestras, contributing a variety of unusual sounds. Probably the best known of these is the Moog Synthesizer, named after its inventor, Robert Moog. The role of electronic instruments is something for the future to determine.

Any large group of performers must have a leader. In orchestral music he is called the conductor. Originally his function was to beat time, and this is still an important part of his job. He also sees to it that all the instruments keep together, that they come in at the proper time, and that a balance is maintained among the different sections. The conductor also controls the tempo (speed) and the volume at which the orchestra plays.

In other words, while each player must contribute his own skills to the performance, it is the conductor's job to blend them all together.

The conductor and the orchestra usually hold many rehearsals before they present a work in public. They go over individual parts and then put the whole piece together. During the rehearsals there may be discussions and questions. Once the concert has started, the conductor is the boss.

Conductor

A young man once went up to the great conductor Arthur Nikisch and said "Please teach me to conduct." Nikisch replied: "Of course, I'd be glad to. It's easy: 1-2-3-4, 1-2-3, 1-2. The rest you have to do yourself."

EUGENE ORMANDY
in an interview (1969)

During a performance, the conductor indicates his wishes to the orchestra through gestures. He usually holds a short stick called a baton in his right hand to make his signals easier to follow. The right hand gives the time pattern, counting out the number of beats in each measure. The left hand indicates the more subtle shadings and stresses.

The conductor should have an understanding of all the instruments in the orchestra. He should know their capability and color. He should also have the ability to work with members of the orchestra in a firm but friendly fashion, so that everybody will always play his best, yet remain a part of the ensemble.

Finally, the conductor should be a profound student of music, so as to understand what a composer intended to say. To re-create the composer's meaning and message is the joint task of the conductor and the orchestra.

The world has come a long way since the Earl of Chester-field warned his son against playing a musical instrument for his pleasure or his profit. Boys and girls today are doing it for both. Making music has become an enjoyable, useful activity for more young people than ever before.

They begin for different reasons and at different ages. Some young people seem to be innately musical and begin playing the piano or another instrument by themselves. Others do so because their parents want them to. While some of these drop out after a while, many who stick to it find they like making music and are grateful for the parental pressure that got them started.

More and more youngsters today are receiving their first musical exposure in school, where they are "given" an instrument by a teacher. Orchestra and band training is spreading rapidly in American school systems, providing musical instruction that previous generations lacked. Learning to enjoy an instrument, which used to be a privilege reserved for a few, is now an opportunity open to practically everyone.

Which instrument should you select? That is a question which each individual must of course decide for himself, usually with the help of a parent or a teacher. One person may have a natural feel for the drums, another for the piano. Some may be more at home with a stringed instrument; others may prefer blowing into a trumpet or clarinet. Listening carefully for a period of time to the various instruments may help you decide which you would like to play. It also might be useful to talk it over with friends who already play in an orchestra, or even to try handling the various instruments yourself a little bit.

Should you be a certain age to play an instrument? Generally speaking, it's not crucial—any time is a good time to begin. But with certain instruments, such as the piano and the violin, the earlier the better. These require hours of practice to develop the necessary dexterity and control. Although there are notable exceptions, pianists and string players usually start their studies at a fairly early age—in extreme cases six or seven.

Woodwind and brass players generally begin later. Many

Finale

If you love music, hear it; go to operas, concerts, and pay fiddlers to play for you; but I insist upon your neither piping nor fiddling yourself. It puts a gentleman in a very frivolous, contemptible light.

LORD CHESTERFIELD
in a letter to his son (April 19, 1749)

young children simply lack the wind capacity and the lip control necessary to command a true orchestral instrument. But once they begin, they develop rapidly. There are some fine young wind musicians in American high school orchestras. The same is true of percussionists, some of whom first make their talents known in kindergarten rhythm bands!

Not all instruments are equally easy. The violin, as noted, requires years of hard work. Among the woodwinds, the double reeds (oboes and bassoons) seem to present more problems than the single reeds (clarinet and saxophone). The flute *embouchure* is difficult to master, and it's necessary to develop the proper "lip" to play all the brasses. But no one who really wants to play an instrument will let technical challenges stand in the way. They all can be overcome—and have been by thousands of young people.

It used to be that certain instruments were regarded as suitable for girls and others for boys. But as a glance around any high school orchestra will tell you, sex distinctions are out. There are female trumpeters and percussionists, male harpists and flutists. It's a rare school group that doesn't have representatives of both sexes in virtually all sections. Women make up an ever increasing proportion of the nation's professional orchestras.

Naturally, a beginning musician will do most of his playing and practicing at the outset by himself. But it shouldn't be too long before he's ready to begin playing with others. The sooner the better, because ensemble playing is one of the greatest of all musical experiences. A violinist or cellist can team up with a pianist to try out a simple sonata. Any string player worth his rosin likes nothing better than to get together with other string players for an evening of quartet playing. Woodwind or brass players can join to play some of the surprisingly rich repertory that has been written for wind ensembles made up of all sorts of instrumental combinations. And of course, at the summit is the greatest ensemble of all, the symphony orchestra.

It used to be that few ever began their musical studies with the idea they might end up playing in an orchestra. The serious young musician usually dreamed of becoming a soloist. His ambition was to stand front and center on the stage at Carnegie Hall while the audience cheered and the critics rushed off to write reviews hailing the newest prodigy. Merely to play in an orchestra was regarded as a confession of failure and a form of drudgery.

Now all that has changed. The symphony orchestra has become a symbol of the cultural eminence of this country. According to the American Symphony Orchestra League, there now are 1,531 orchestras in the United States. Of these, 290 are college and university orchestras, and 1,100 are community orchestras, most of whose members are musicians by avocation. Of the others, 113 are metropolitan or urban orchestras, made up nearly entirely of professionally-trained musicians, and 28 are major, or completely professional in make-up. In addition, there are countless high school and junior high orchestras and bands.

What this means is that orchestras exist on all levels of skill. Many of them are eager to have young musicians join up and partake in the sheer pleasure of playing.

Along with the increase in orchestras a growth in size and understanding on the part of the audience has taken place. More people are listening to good music today than ever before. They appreciate fine playing in the concert hall, and in the school auditorium.

The result is that orchestral musicians, especially in the leading organizations, are universally respected for their skill and knowledge. They have a strong union and have won many improvements in their working conditions. More than in any previous era, they are well-paid and secure.

Most important, whether they play for their livelihood or for recreation, they find abiding satisfaction in their work. Symphonic music is, after all, one of man's noblest achievements. It expresses his loftiest ideals and deepest emotions. That is why so many people have made it part of their lives. "All musical people seem to be happy," said the British writer Sydney Smith. "It is to them the engrossing pursuit; almost the only innocent and unpunished passion."

At the end of the rainbow of sound the legendary pot of gold may not await you. But you will find there a reward even richer and more enduring.

A Note on Recordings

Records are a pleasant and convenient way of becoming acquainted at home with the sounds of the instruments. In fact, several composers have written symphonic pieces designed to introduce listeners to the various components of the orchestra.

Serge Prokofiev's *Peter and the Wolf*, available in many recordings, is one of the best. It has a delightful story, and a narrator indicates how each character is represented by an instrument—the bird by a flute, the duck by an oboe, the grandfather by a bassoon, and Peter by a string quartet.

Benjamin Britten's *Young Person's Guide to the Orchestra* performs the same service, a bit more seriously. Here the instruments take turns playing variations on a theme by the seventeenth-century British composer Henry Purcell. There also is a narration, but in some recordings it is omitted.

Camille Saint-Saëns's *Carnival of the Animals* is a fun piece. The composer subtitled it "Grand Zoological Fantasy." Various instruments impersonate animals—such as the double-bass, an elephant and the cello, a swan. However, several important instruments are not represented at all, and some of the musical portraits are left to two pianos.

A number of other frequently recorded works, such as Ravel's *Bolero* and Rimsky-Korsakov's *Capriccio Espagnol*, also are excellent instrumental display pieces. But perhaps the best way to appreciate what the instruments can do is to listen to them as they make their contribution to standard symphonic literature—the symphonies of Beethoven and Brahms, the tone poems of Richard Strauss, the ballet scores of Stravinsky, and the many other works that have been suggested in this book.

Index of Musical Examples